To Jo

GW00728866

Reeling and Writhing

Barry Smith

With all best wishes

Barry Smith

First Edition 2023

Barry Smith has asserted his authorship and given permission to
Dempsey & Windle for these poems to be published here.

Published by Dempsey & Windle under their VOLE imprint

15 Rosetrees
Guildford
Surrey
GU1 2HS
UK
01483 571164
dempseyandwindle.com
A catalogue record for this book is available from the British
Library

British Library Cataloguing-in-Publication Data

ISBN: 9781913329914

Cover image:
Detail from Peter Iden's painting *South Downs Summer 2*. With
grateful thanks to the Estate of Peter Iden.
www.peteriden.co.uk

:eling and Writing

:eling and Writing offers a retrospective of Barry Smith's
·iting covering a time frame of over fifty years from the Sixties
 the Twenties. Spinning off ideas and themes of reeling and
 :ithing as suggested by Lewis Carroll's classic *Alice* books, the
)ems consider notions of appearance and reality, of illusion and
 :lusion, of educational aspiration and social manipulation, of
 ,e search for individual truth in a world where little can be taken
)r granted. As well as his epic/satiric take on the pandemic in
 ie award-shortlisted *The Masks of Anarchy,* there are poems on
 ieatre and music, on nature and eco-awareness, on politics and
 onflict, on philosophy and judgement, together with songs
 omposed for Smith's productions of *Alice, The Country of the
 3lind* and the medieval *Mysteries.* As Lewis Carroll would have
 t – of mystery, ancient and modern.

Barry Smith

Barry Smith is the director of the South Downs Poetry Festival
and was the co-ordinator of the Festival of Chichester for ten
years. He curates the poetry element of Blakefest and edits
Poetry & All That Jazz magazine. Smith was runner-up in a BBC
Proms Poetry Competition and shortlisted for the Bread & Roses
Songwriting and Spoken Word Award, 2021. His collection,
Performance Rites (Waterloo Press), was published in 2021. He
has worked in education, as a theatre director and as a critic.
Productions directed include *Antigone* for the Edinburgh Festival
and *Murder in the Cathedral* and *The Mysteries* (Parts I and II,
Creation to Nativity and *Passion to Doomsday)* for Chichester
Cathedral. Smith's poems have appeared in journals and
magazines, as well as online and on YouTube, including *Acumen,
Agenda, Culture Matters, Frogmore Papers, The Journal, The
Stony Thursday Book, London Grip, Orbis, South, Ver Poets,
Littoral Press* and *Poetry South East.* He can sometimes be
caught hobnobbing with jazz and roots musicians as a
performance poet.

Acknowledgements

The Masks of Anarchy, with a musical setting by multi-instrumentalist Charlotte Glasson and filmed by Katie Bennett, was shortlisted for the Culture Matters Bread & Roses Songwriting and Spoken Word Award 2021. The film can be viewed on the South Downs Poetry Festival YouTube channel. It was premiered live at Shout Out for Shelley as part of the Shelley bicentenary celebrations in his hometown of Horsham, Sussex, in 2022. It was impossible to live through the covid pandemic without responding and Shelley's *Masque of Anarchy* provided the inspiration to write. *Silencing* offers a different take on the times. *Route Sixty-Six Revisited* was commissioned for the launch of the Culture Spark festival in the Chichester District in 2022. *The Bargain* was Commended in the Slipstream Poetry Competition 2023. Poems from this collection have also appeared in various guises in *Culture Matters, The Journal, London Grip, Up, Littoral Press, South, Acumen, Frogmore Papers* and *Poetry & All That Jazz* magazines amongst other places.

The song lyrics in Section II, A Looking Glass World, were originally written for my theatre productions of *Alice,* based on the books by Lewis Carroll, staged at the Alexandra Theatre, Bognor Regis; *The Country of the Blind,* based on the short story by H.G. Wells, staged at the Bartlett Hall, Chichester; and *The Mysteries* by Tony Harrison, based on the medieval miracle plays, staged in promenade style at Chichester Cathedral. The songs incorporate some words and phrases from the books.

Although this is a retrospective selection, the poems are not presented in the order they were written but are organised in thematic sections. *Between Dream and Sweetheart* depicts two Ukrainian villages, Mria and Myla, whose names translate as Dream and Sweetheart. *Theresa's Tears* was sparked by a letter from Sasha Simic in The Guardian. *Everything* was inspired by a line from *The Calvary Cross* by Richard Thompson, as quoted in Tony Harrison's playscript *The Mysteries* (Faber). I gratefully acknowledge Richard Thompson's permission to include words from the song. *Decline and Fall* is a largely found poem, using words and phrases from the journals of Marco Polo and Dr S. W. Bushell, as quoted in *In Xanadu, a Quest*, by William Dalrymple (Flamingo Books). Thanks to David Godwin Associates for permission to include this material. *Conditional Tense* is a fictional dramatic monologue and does not depict any living persons. The epigraph to *Be What You Would Seem to Be* is taken from a speech by the Duchess in *Alice in Wonderland* by Lewis Carroll.

I acknowledge support and inspiration from my family and from my long-term collaborators in assorted arts projects, especially with theatre productions and the South Downs Poetry Festival. I would like to pay tribute to two inspirational English lecturers for giving me a lifelong love of poetry, Joe Grady at Mander College, Bedford and Francis Doherty at Keele University.

Huge thanks to everyone who has inspired and encouraged me over the years – you know who you are and how much I owe to all of you.

Thanks to the editor and publisher of my previous collection: ***Performance Rites* (Waterloo Press, 2021)**

BTS 2023.

'I couldn't afford to learn it,' said the Mock Turtle with a sigh. 'I only took the regular course.'

'What was that?' inquired Alice.

'Reeling and Writhing, of course, to begin with,' the Mock Turtle replied; 'and then the different branches of Arithmetic — Ambition, Distraction, Uglification, and Derision.'

'What else had you to learn?'

'Well, there was Mystery,' the Mock Turtle replied, counting off the subjects on his flappers, '— Mystery, ancient and modern...'.

— **Lewis Carroll**, *Alice's Adventures in Wonderland.*

CONTENTS

I – Waiting in the Wings

II – A Looking Glass World
Songs from *Alice*, *The Country of the Blind* and *The Mysteries*

Alice

The Country of the Blind

The Mysteries

III – The Ghost in the Machine

I – Waiting in the Wings

Radioactive

That guy will burn himself out before he's thirty,
observed Professor Burkhardt, the bow-tied
consultant psychiatrist, in his best
clinical manner to his wife Brenda,
the strict English mistress who rarely gave
a student a grade higher than a C,

because, she said, they could always do better.
I didn't get his diagnosis at the time,
standing on stage with my cast, the Jets and Sharks,
riding the applause for West Side Story
which had just reached its tear-stained climax
in the new community college hall.

He was almost correct in his judgement
as I winged my way on a prayer through
Ernie's Incredible Illucinations,
placing spies and dead soldiers in the surgery
and cavorting in the Three Cripples bar
with Nancy, Bill Sykes and bottles of gin,

toasting Oliver and the Artful Dodger
and belting out As Long as He Needs Me
for a sentimentally inclined crowd.
But somehow, turned upside down for screening
with radioisotopes of barium meal
highlighting the stations of the tube-map,

I came through it all with just a warning
to take things easier in the rehearsal room
before my incipient ulcer burst.
Instead, I conjured castles in the air,
taking six stitches on the head and bleeding
all over the set of the Dark of the Moon.

Up the Ladder

That summer, on the brush with Bruce
tarting up the paintwork on village
council estates in Bedfordshire,

we were summoned one hot afternoon
by a toot from a passing white van –
the driver had spotted two likely lads

up the ladder with dangling paint pots.
Winding down the driver's window
and resting his elbow on the doorframe,

he beckoned us to the kerbside.
'Ere, he said, sliding the words from
the corner of his mouth, real spiv style,

'ere lads, wanna buy a nice watch?
With a deft flourish, he pushed up
his shirt sleeve to whisk into view

half a dozen watches, gleaming gold
with metal straps and shiny dials.
I can let you have them cheap, he said,

they fell off the back of a lorry.
We admired, smiled and declined,
being familiar with the Jack-the-Lad

traders peddling their wares – *'ave a look!*
'ave a look! – calling across Saturday
market stalls on country town squares.

Not to be deterred he swiftly quipped,
what about a gift for your girlfriend then?
and rolling back the other shirtsleeve he flashed

a jauntily bejewelled array of bracelets.
Well, we knew all about these chaps, we'd seen
them growing up, at the Empire and the Regal,

silver-screened, sharply suited spivs, larger
than life small time crooks from Brighton Rock,
so we returned to our piecework painting –

there was good money to be had if you were quick
as we blazed on site in our elderly flash cars,
Bruce's yellow Lotus and my Cortina GT –

but the work dried up as winter drew in
and we returned to our other lives, me back
to teaching while Bruce drifted to the gay scene

in London town, chasing the high time on
a different kind of spree, until the AIDS
epidemic knocked him off his chosen ladder.

Warrior

They don't make men like Mad Jack anymore,
maybe that's a good thing, I don't know,
but when the autumn storms drive the brigantine
onto the splintering rocks at Brook Chine

and Henri et Leontine lies broken-backed,
rudder gone with all spars cast overboard
and when the lifeboat crew are driven back
by the lambasting waves and all looks lost,

Jack Seely grabs a last-ditch line of hope,
dives into the buckling, salt-sucking waves
and shepherds the battered men ashore
to shelter in the great barn at Mottistone;

now the symbiotic figurehead
of Henri et Leontine in close embrace
graces the charity bookshop wall in the manor
where you can browse and read of Jack's heroics

astride his bay thoroughbred horse Warrior,
cantering through falling shells at the Somme,
floundering through the mud at Passchendaele
and defying the strafing machine gun fire,

you understand that to ride together
leading the charge at Moreuil Wood
demands a grudging kind of homage
for a will that will not bend to circumstance,

that will accept the impossible odds
cresting the flood of tides or artillery shells,
headlong or headstrong, who can say,
but man and horse through fire and water

will have their way and leave their mark on the day.

The Wild Garlic at Shorwell

The path winds through the starry banks
of hydra-headed wild white garlic
sparkling with dew in the morning light;
swishing through the cascading leaves
lifting the spiky brambles with a cane,
you follow the curving line to the bridge,
a rustic, trellised, wooden relic spanning
the country lane to Shorwell village.

From here you catch the echoes of the past,
the maroon liveried, split windscreen
Matador gun tractor from Brook guarding
a yard of abandoned trailers and ploughs;
walk on through angelica, white myrtle
and cranesbill to the greystone churchyard,
where, across the lane and over the stream
the path leads to the manor of Northcourt.

And listen, that's the piping of the organ
swelling through the oak and marble hall
where Mary in a silk indigo gown
plays for Swinburne sitting at her side,
prompting imagery of golden apples
for Atalanta in Calydon, leaning
together in a shaft of light, breathing
intimacies of metrical discourse

learned on the flogging block at Eton,
the sharp pleasures and pains of rods,
the embodiment of the aesthetic,
the thwack and thrum swishing through hand
and heart, illuminating the sufferings,
the sensuous chastisement of the birch,
the footsteps running free through the waves
of wild white garlic frothing the winding path.

Silencing

I remember Eyam,
not for anything specific,
no dramatic discovery
of the boundary stone
where coins were placed
in vinegar to pay
for food and essentials
from the outside world
when the village turned
its back in self-isolation,
locked itself down
to contain and confront
the escalating plague –
no, it was the absences
I found remarkable,
the absolute quiet,
the total stillness
in the green churchyard,
no whirr of machinery
or buzz of traffic,
no birdsong,
as if the village still
contained the imprint
of all that sickness,
all that death.

I had taught the story
A Parcel of Patterns
to rapt students learning
how the latest London fashions,
the twirl or drape or bow,
had brought death to Eyam –
I had not expected to live it,
to find myself transported,
to walk the streets with masks,

to cross the road or step
warily aside from
approaching figures,
and I cannot help but recall
that half-forgotten
weekend visit to Eyam
as I look out today over
the chalk escarpment
of the Trundle at Goodwood,
with its breath-taking views
over the deserted racecourse,
like some mysterious
archaeological domain,
puzzling evidence
of a lost civilization
like the horse-slaughter pit
of early homo-sapiens
at nearby Boxgrove.

You can walk around
the ramparts of the iron-age fort,
you can see the twisted remnants
of the world-war two bunkers,
the rusty wire fences,
crumbling concrete blocks,
masts, aerials, brambles;
you can look out over the sea
as mist swathes the harbour,
the rivulets and inlets
silvery reflections in a haze
of shapeless buildings and trees,
nature putting us back
into our limited space
with the trilling skylark's song,
the intricate staccatos,
flutters and sudden swoops.

And there at the heart
of the walled Roman city
of Chichester, I see
the solitary ascent
of the cathedral spire
asserting its due prominence,
claiming the cityscape,
and then I think
of the silence of Eyam,
of the returning quiet
when the skylarks settle,
I think of the old press reports
of startled observers
leaning from leather-strapped
windows of nineteenth
century railway carriages
as the lofty spire gave way,
crumpled into the lead roof,
crumbling into smoke and dust
filling the nave with
motes of suspended light

and the aftermath of silence,
always the silence.

Spillage

Ventnor Botanic Gardens
(site of the National Chest Hospital, dismantled)

The water runs through my hands
spilling from the lip of the bowl,
glancing on the handkerchief
white petals of waxen waterlilies.
Around me rare specimens
are photographed and catalogued,
trophies for dusty albums,
as wisteria Alba tendrils drift
embracing a shady shelter.

I am lulled by the water
and the sun, botanic beauties
abound, but the graces of the garden
are compromised by the past:
here is the site of surrender
where dark red globules splattered
pressed white napkins and sheets,
consuming all who wasted and watched
the frothy fountains running dry.

Willows

After Ivon Hitchens

sometimes
you can hear the voices in the woods
sighing by a sycamore tree
singing of a green willow
streams of light filtering the riverbed
the tangled pool, the linear stretch
the gate between shadowed waters
the path, the leaf, the veins
the patterned willow boughs
gently curling grey-green leaves
flowing from olive-brown arcing stems
sometimes
you can see the music in the woods

Brook Churchyard

Scoured stone, moss-steeped cross and darkling yew,
solitary sentinel gazing with hooded eyes
over burnished sea, crumbling cliff, opalescent sky,
restful chapel dozing on the mount of sorrow,
how many have lain in your soothing arms
seeking easeful succour from your supine breast
and still recline, languorously, through lost centuries?
At the taut turning point where coffins unload,
steadying hands shift the fretful weight,
with shuffling progress impel brass and oak
through whorling wind, sharp sun, slow-seeping rain
or indifferent cloud, grey piled upon ashen grey;
you lie with pliant portals, soft fissures of earth
and leavened nave, transepts wide-spreading, embracing
flesh and dust and all.

Time and Tide
Totland, Isle of Wight

We track onwards deep into the undercliff
where light flickers and dapples the mossy rocks,
catches the fringes of filigree ferns,
while sharp evergreen tongues lick the soft air
above all-encompassing ivy leaf
stretching to nudge bush and stone, plant and tree
into its enfolding, deep-green embrace.
Fragments of light catch the whirring wings
of hovering flies in staccato streams,
lacing incalculable aery patterns
amongst the drowsy, curtaining creepers.
Through this lush-shuttered primeval domain
we drift, encapsulated, protected
from intrusion and even, perhaps, from ourselves.

And so we break through to the high heathland
awash with purple waves of wiry heather,
threaded with carmine pink spikes, bright rosebay
willowherb and scented, scrambling yellow-white
honeysuckle tendrils intermingling
with prickly gorse, braving the seasonal
winds which today are but a wisping breeze.
We feel the pulse of the sea and the earth,
around and below, while above, the sky
seeps from a painterly blue to pewter;
stippled streaks of luminescent clouds drift,
overarching the arms of the stretching cliffs,
reflecting in the wash of the reclining bay.

Here, where all is held in a glazed stasis,
there is a trinity of displacement:
to our right, the mainland lines the horizon
dotted with remnants of abandoned forts;
to our left, the Needles thrust their sharpened
stones above the encircling, abrasive sea
forever washing at their rocky roots;
and straight ahead, where the patient kestrel
hovers, lies the nurturing mound which housed
the Bronze Age dwellers of Headon Warren,
lost now to the vagrant vicissitudes
of tribal or elemental struggle.

Supplicant

As if called to midday prayer he hunches
on all fours, his back turned to the abbey

where angels and pilgrims blithely
ascend heavenwards gripping stone ladders

flanking iron-studded oak doors
while solemn attendants collect entrance fees.

The crouching man kneels in convocation,
vision fully engaged with grey pavement

as a blackly bristling wire-haired terrier
stands guarding his singularly suppliant master,

sole immobility in this crush of busy shoppers
hustling beneath civic Roman colonnade

rising in fluted stonework above.
No-one pauses or seems to witness,

no hasty handful of change clinks by his side,
only the pool of liquid spreads

slowly suppurating the patch
between recusant dog and man.

Ducking and Diving

They said work hard, keep your head down and you'll get on,
so he did, kept his head down and his working neat,
always finishing first, turning with a sense of unrestraint
to the book, King Solomon's Mines or Prester John, in his desk.

At the little school he was subdued, lost in lines of chairs,
but after he failed the eleven plus, they gave the remnants
a stiff Darwinian test, which he passed and rose
step by step each year to the top of the top class.

But he baulked the thirteen plus and the headmaster's daughter
went up to the grammar school, so they said, in his place,
though gradually his head came up and he looked
the teachers in the eye and progressed to the tech college,

holding his own in the debates, keeping on against the odds
until he was given his teaching certificate, approved,
so he thought at last, just keeping on with lessons
but now sitting on the other side of the invisible line,

keeping their heads down to work hard, be neat, get on,
ducking and diving round the snares strewn in their path,
like mallards upending to reconnoitre what lies beneath,
or frogmen negotiating jagged splines of rusty wrecks.

Theresa's Tears

Theresa saw the signs
and they were dark

she shed a little tear
when she saw the exit poll
on election night

but the tears she did not shed
tell a bitter tale

no tears for the lost
in the Calais holding camps
no tears for the nurses
for the teachers and firefighters
who felt the squeeze of pay restraint
but not the holding of hands

no tears for the refugees
for whom we could find no room
no tears for those removed
discreetly from benefits
to helpfully die on the job

and no tears for those who
fled the Grenfell Tower inferno

Theresa shed a little tear
but it was not shed for us.

Are the Macbeths alive and well and living in N.E. Asia?

Remember how it goes –
the castle is surprised
and everyone put to the sword,
wife and children and all the babes.

Or then again, a quiet word –
is it far that you journey today,
and goes your son with you?
But fail not our banquet tonight.

Nor fail our father's funeral rites,
but the general is surprised,
carousing not deep mourning
at the old tyrant's passing.

Nor incur the jealous wrath
of the fiery, queenly consort
by singing songs of dark horsewomen
amongst bright hymns of patriotic praise.

So the families are all gathered,
marshalled to witness the set-piece passing,
machine-gunned against the barracks wall
or obliterated by brute mortar fall.

Remember how it goes –
the castle is surprised
and everyone put to the sword,
wife and children and all the babes.

Separate Ways
The London Tube Bombings, 7.7.05

It begins with a game of cricket in the park,
the comforting thwack of willow on leather,
subtle deceptions of devious spin
or full-blooded roar of scorching pace,
of lofted bat acknowledging applause.

From there we have to find a place on this
seventh day of the seventh month for modern
inconveniences, traffic congestion
and short-changing attendants at those crossroads
of contemporary civilization,
the motorway service station.

But then, there's a certain nostalgic redress
entering the portals of a main-line station,
boarding the inter-city express laden
with commuters, clerks and travellers
flooding the capital's busy routines.

And so we have the parting of the ways,
the last farewells of firebrand fellowship,
weighty burdens borne in separate directions,
just a minor hold-up with a cancelled connection
and a trip to McDonalds for a solitary last supper
before detonating the first bus home.

Decline and Fall

broken stairways   griffons
and the   tangled remains
of sculpted   marble monuments
litter   the ground
in   every   direction
with looping briar   undergrowth
in   distant   echo
of that   paradigm
where
the tall and   rolling grasses
vacantly   stretch
et cetera

dank weeds   fox burrows
and the   haunting cry
of calling   owls and night birds
scarce   one stone
now   canted   above another
with truncated   columns
in   distant   echo
of that   paradigm
where
gilded and carved   arches delight
sensuously   astonish
et cetera

The Chances

'Chance and money rule the world'– Christian Martin

in the cellar
             murky air susurrates
as the oscillating coin
                spins and swirls
eyes and hopes
           heads   and heads again

in the cinema
              angled light implicates
as the revolving chamber
                stills and spurns
eyes and hopes
           click   and click again

in the hospital
              strictured time enervates
as the hairspring trigger
                shapes and stalls
hopes and eyes
           flinch   and flinch again

Between Worlds
JMW Turner – Chichester Canal

This is where the artist held his sketchbook,
suspended somewhere between the two banks
and gazing ahead into the sunset over
the blue-grey downs, the water translucent,
silvered with reflected light, the rigging
of a brig holding the vanishing point,
a barque tucked into one bank, casting off,
and three poplar trees drawing the eye
to the cathedral spire floating on the horizon.

Today, I stand where Turner stood on the apex
of Hunston bridge, seeing and not seeing
the sights he saw on Chichester canal,
then the marvel of the modern age, now
a tourist trail with a gauche reproduction
of his vision tacked onto the balustrade.
On this cusp of another spring, angelica,
red campion and white meadowsweet are
hibernating, soon to share their blessing.

And on another day, on another bridge,
in suspension over Bedford river,
I gaze ahead to the spire of St Paul's Church
spiking the sharp, bright autumn skies, with clouds
of ruddy-golden-brown beech leaves lining the banks,
and think of my mother adrift on a bed of white,
her breathing seeping away, blending into
the air, like the smoke from Turner's engine
bridging the worlds of Rain, Steam and Speed.

Figures in a Sussex Landscape
or 'Figs from Thistles' – Alfred, Lord Tennyson

It's an odd sight, not what you would expect
on a damp and dirty November morning
with the trees still dripping spools of moisture.

He looks like a gentleman, but hot and flustered,
the shoulder cape of his dark Inverness coat
flapping in the coiling gusts and eddies.

Madam is sitting stiffly, awkwardly,
as he pushes her forwards with a grimace,
the wheels of the Bath chair sticking in the mud.

She tugs at the ties of the neat white bonnet,
contrasting with the crammed opulence
of his wide-awake, broad brimmed hat cresting

dark locks shaking free to brush the straggling beard
and scarf, wisping in the chilly air of unkempt lanes,
where the landscape is scarred by signs of the storm;

some trees are down, an elm and an ash sprawled
at angles, snagging twigs and branches impeding
the couple as he glances back at the louring house

with chipped roofing tiles splattered and dotted around.
We have, he says darkly, such a peck of troubles,
you might as well get figs from thistles

as sense from me on this ill-omened day.
She sighs and proffers a flickering smile
as they push on down the lanes, abandoning

the wreckage and storm-blown damage of their house,
with the bedroom wall blown down, revealing
the legacy of an old Roman Catholic chapel,

as the wind roared through the gaps, water rushing
over dining room furniture, washing at the stains
of a baby's burial place, seeping into every crack.

It's not what a poet expects from his longed-for
rural retreat, away from the clamour of the crowds
sucking the life-force from his pen and his brow.

Barflies
i.m. Mike Grace, innkeeper, the Crown, Shorwell, IOW

Like insects each with distinctive carapace
flashing green, black and blue iridescence,
the barflies hover, darting gnomic glances
from gleaming brass hand pumps to diamond glasses.

Beetle-black with elbows angularly
possessing the time-smoothed bar, the old lag rests,
solemnly supping his elixir, Flowers best,
frothing in engraved cut-glass familiar mug,

while with seething energy, the wise acre
from Wichita, exotic migrant species,
buzzes and poses, seeking any slight chance
to swoop and launch antennae-fizzing barbs.

In the corner, tucked behind a barrel seat,
a red-veined gourmand steadily munches,
metronomically liquefying his private feast.
With whippet-thin limbs telescopically

juggling ashtrays, empties and a thin cigar,
the master of ceremonies hazily drifts
through swirling blue smoke with proprietorial grace,
king of the barflies in this booze-hallowed space.

Quarantined

Remember the SARS epidemic,
the covid pandemic lockdown
and the panic over Ebola,
travellers in isolation camps,
face masks and rubber gloves,
lateral flow testing kits,
keep out notices, wire fences,
special checks at customs?

Well, I've been mail swept,
protectively cut adrift,
placed in virtual quarantine.
So, I pick up the phone
and call the council offices.
You've choked off my message
I say, put me in limbo
as if I'm infectious –

I'm afraid you are, sir, he says,
we monitor all incoming mail,
you've got a high profanity index.
That's absurd, I tell the man,
you've censored my email,
cut off my communication
about the city arts festival,
it's bonkers, what's profane about that?

Well, let me see, I'll check by
clicking on the screen in the office;
it's the poetry, it says here,
'Poems of love and desire.'
So, there we have it, official,
poetry is infectious, dangerous,
and the old Dylan song it seems is right:
love is just a four-letter word.

Waiting in the Wings

Beginners please!

The stage manager's urgent summons
calls us from the Green Room
to a state of readiness in our allotted places,
upstage right and downstage left,
waiting for that line or musical phrase,
our cue to enter bringing the latest news
setting in action that spiral of events,
that careless interruption or unfortunate complication
resulting in accusations, shouts, shots or laughter.
Until then we wait with decisions taken from us,
our deterministic universe fixed in the rehearsal room
offering only the illusion of alternative possibilities;
this state of limbo is a world unto itself,
we spend our time patiently listening
or impatiently pacing up and down,
according to our mood or our nature.

Vivien is a method actor deep in the interior world
of her present character, her body shaped by the text,
that moment of loss in her childhood
traced in the angle of chin or elbows.
She'll not see you there or hear you whisper
unless you remind her of her father.
Tony retreats to the gents and chants in the stalls
lubricating his vowels, 'Me-me-me-me-me-meeeee…'
Susie and Andrew are lost in their mirrors
with eyeliners, latex and powder,
Richard watches wide-eyed, learning the ropes and tropes.
Mark is plotting jokes – when you discover his body
later in act three sprawled on the carpet
upstage and unseen by the audience,
he'll roll his eyes and stick out his tongue,
the laughing corpse to make you corpse.

Rowan is bitching and dissing the crew,
Michael is leaning in and chatting up the girls,
his fingers lightly brushing hair or patting bums;
and then there are the crafty smokers
pacing the corridors and reciting their lines,
nervous energy splattering like steam on the walls.

And so each actor plays their part
until the last syllable of recorded script
when the lights dim for the curtain call,
preferably well before closing time in the bar…

Last orders please!

II – A Looking Glass World

Songs from *Alice, The Country of the Blind* and *The Mysteries*

Songs from *Alice*

Falling
Down the rabbit hole

Down, down, down
Falling through the world
Sliding down the sides
Twisting in the air
Sinking through the earth

Falling like a stone
Sinking into space
Twirling like a leaf
Floating in the earth

Falling…floating…
Twisting…twirling…
Sinking…
Down, down, down
Falling through the world

Down, down, down
Tumbling down the hole
Squirming like a worm
Burrowing like a mole
Miles beneath the earth

Down, down, down
Rolling like a ball
Cruising like a bat
Flying in the dark
Falling through the world

Down, down, down
Down.

Do Cats Eat Bats

Dinah, my dear
I wish you were here,
No mice in the air
No birds in the earth.

Do cats eat bats?
Do bats eat cats?
Do gnats chew mats?
Do mats gnaw gnats?
Do mice like hats?
Do cats eat bats?

Dinah, my dear
I wish you were here,
To pet and to purr
To smooth your soft fur.

Do cats eat bats?
Do bats chase rats?
Do cats like moles?
To chase down holes?
Do rats chase cats?
Do cats eat bats?

Dinah, my dear
I wish you were here,
To nurse in my arms
To keep me from harm.

Shrinking

I'm growing……
Smaller by the minute
Smaller with each second
Shrinking closer to the ground
Every part of everything
Is whirling round and round.

Shrinking! Shrinking!
Smaller than a sparrow
Faster than an arrow
Zooming! Zooming!
Compressing down and down
Chin will soon be landing
Plonk upon the ground.

Small is beautiful
Titchy's wonderful
Teeny's fabulous
Tiny's tremendous
Shrinking! Shrinking!
S…H…R…I…N…K…I…N…G!

Have you ever wondered
What it would be like
To join the birds and bees
And be smaller than your knees?

Telescoping down
Rushing to the ground
Stars and earth are turning
Fire and air are churning
Whirling round and round.

Shrinking! Shrinking!
Shrinking! Shrinking!
S…H…R…I…N…K…I…N…G!

Now all tiny creatures
Open wide their eyes
See the new arrival
Much reduced in size.

I'm growing……
Smaller by the minute,
Smaller with each second
Shrinking closer to the ground
Every part of everything
Is whirling round and round.

Small is beautiful
Titchy's wonderful
Teeny's fabulous
Tiny's tremendous

Shrinking! Shrinking!
S
   H
     R
       I
         N
           K
             I
               N
                 G!

The Cheshire Cat's Mad Song

You must be mad, as mad as a bat
Or you wouldn't come here, don't you know that?

Well, a dog's not mad, you'll grant me that
Though he jumps and jiggles and knocks you flat,
But when he's cross, he'll bark and he'll growl,
He'll snarl and he'll bite with a frightening howl!

Now a happy dog will wag his tail
And wriggle his ears, not bark or howl,
But when I'm pleased, I menace and growl,
It's when I'm angry that I wag my tail.

You must be mad, as mad as a bat,
Or you wouldn't come here, don't you know that?
Mad, mad, mad as a bat!
Mad, mad as a Cheshire Cat! Gggrrrrrr!

Dream Child

Dream child
Child of the morning
Dream child
Star of the evening
Dreaming so free.

Through misty webs of magic lands
With rainbow colours in your hands
In streams of light and amber seas
You wander through our fantasies.

Dream child
Child of the dream time
Sign of the morning
Light of a lifetime
Roaming so free.

In courts of kings and fearsome queens
In wondrous games of chequered play
Near magic plants and pools of tears
You fly beyond all earthly dreams.

Dream child
Child of the morning
Dream child
Star of the evening
Dreaming so free.

In forest places dark and green
With strangest creatures of your dreams
You bring your bright and gentle ways
To echo with your laughing tears.

Dream child
Child of the dream time
Sign of the morning
Dream child
Light of a lifetime
Beyond all worldly dreams.

Changing Places
The Mad Hatter's Tea Party

When you're sat at a place
When you're stuck in a rut
You look all around you –
And see what others have got!
The grass is much greener
The sky is much bluer
The chair is much softer
The fruit is much fresher
Everything you see is –
Better and betterer!

When you're in this state
Don't argue with fate
Jump onto your feet
And push aside
The people you meet!

Changing places
Changing places…

On your marks and – leave your bases
Raise the standard – flag the races
Pound your feet and – show your paces
Top of the heap – shove your cases
Be aggressive – thump their faces
Changing places – changing places!

No etiquette – forget your graces
Don't be modest – bust your laces
Forget the rules – break the traces
Show your mettle – wave your maces
No holds barred – squash their faces!

Changing places!
Changing places...
Places, places, places...
Changing – places!

When you're sat at a place
When you're stuck in a rut
You look all around you –
And see what others have got!
The cream is much creamier
The jam is much jammier
The juice is much juicier
The tea is much wetter
Everything you see is –
Better and betterer!

When you're in this state
Don't argue with fate
Jump onto your feet
And push aside
The people you meet!

Changing places
Changing places
Changing...
Places...
Places, places, places...
Changing places!

The Song of the Flowers

In winter when the winds do blow
The land is dark and drear and sad,
We hide our heads beneath the snow,
The trees are bare and sigh with cold.

Winter is the dark time,
Winter is the hard time,
The bleak and black and drear time,
We hide beneath the snow.

In spring when buds begin to show
The land is clean and sharp and green,
Daffodils wave to and fro,
The earth is bursting with new life.

Spring is the bright time,
Spring is the birth time,
The new and fresh and clear time,
We dance upon the earth.

In summer when the sun does shine
The land is warm and lush and full,
Larkspur and rosebud are the sign,
The garden is like a bride arrayed.

Summer is the light time,
Summer is the joy time,
The warm and fine and high time,
We sing throughout the land.

In autumn when the leaves do fall
The land is rich and red of hue,
The fruit is ripe but swallows call
To warn of frost upon the soil.

Autumn is the rich time,
Autumn is the juice time,
The sweet and sour change time,
We sing a sad lament.

The Executioner's Rag

Off with his head!
Off with her head!
Off with their heads!
Off with our heads?!

I've got to – roll up my sleeves
I've got to – rub down my block
I've got to – sharpen my axe
You've got to – lose all you've got!

Do the Executioner's Rag!

I pick up my axe and I whirl it and twirl it around
I climb on the scaffold and dare them to utter a sound
They're shaking and quaking knowing they soon will be dead
For my beautiful axe will so lovingly strike off their heads.

I am the king of the axe
I am the chopper of heads
I am the ender of dreams
I am the bringer of screams.

Oooh! He's so big
Oooh! He's so fierce
Oooh! He's the man
With the chopper!

As long as it's not
Your head on the block
Pass around the sandwiches
Knock back the champagne
Enjoy the spectacle –
Do come again.

He's the king of the axe
He's the chopper of heads
He's the ender of dreams
He's the bringer of screams.

Blood is my trademark
Death is my game
Nothing pleases me more
Than gallons of gore.

Off with his head!
Off with her head!
Off with their heads!
Off with our heads?!

Oh, there's nothing I like better
Than buckets and buckets of blood!

Be What You Would Seem to Be

*...Never imagine yourself not to be otherwise than what it
might appear to others that what you were or might have been
was not otherwise than what you had been would have
appeared to them to be otherwise...!*

Be what you would seem to be,
Let others see just who you are,
Speak your mind and you can see
There's no-one like you, near or far.

Be what you would seem to be,
Don't hide your light from anyone,
Let it shine then you can see
That you are you, a special one.

Be true to you and you will see
Through shifting webs of fantasy,
Never doubt that you can be
A touchstone of reality.

Even when the world is changing
And you don't know where you are,
Though the earth spins fast around you
Hold on tight to who you are.

Be true to you and you will see
Through shifting webs of fantasy,
Never doubt that you can be
A touchstone of reality.

Wonderland

Will I ever understand
The wonders of this wonderland?
For every turn I seem to take
Brings further choices I must make.

With racing heart and searching hand
I stumble on through wonderland,
Each corner turned brings wonders new,
Inviting pathways to pursue.

How can I ever understand
The miracles of this wonderland?
Daisies singing, turtles weeping,
Brothers fighting, eagles swimming…

Who could possibly believe
Stories of this wonderland?

Dashing lorries, tumbling lizards,
Grunting babies, dancing lobsters…
Can I hope to understand
The mysteries of this wonderland?

Is it possible to grasp
The nature of my questing task,
Why every creature seems to sing
And tales of joy and sadness bring?

Each corner turned brings wonders new
And further pathways to pursue,
Will I ever understand
The wonders of this wonderland?

A Looking Glass World

Stories for Alice, strange but true,
Reflections of starlight drifting by,
Haunted by creatures lost from view,
Picture book colours flood the sky.

In a looking glass world
Nothing ever stands still,
In a looking glass world
Can it really be true?
In a looking glass,
In a looking glass world.

Stories for Alice, rainbow hue
Flowers and oysters sadly sigh,
Magical creatures dance for you,
Fantasy figures whispering by.

In a looking glass world
Dreams can sometimes come true,
In a looking glass world
Can you believe your eyes?
In a looking glass,
In a looking glass world.

Stories for Alice, told for you,
Gryphons and dodos sadly sigh,
Mystical creatures dance for you,
Shadows of starlight drifting by.

In a looking glass world
Nothing ever stands still,
In a looking glass world
Can it really be true?
In a looking glass,
In a looking glass world.

Songs from *The Country of the Blind*

Earthquake

The ground shakes
The stones move
And branches tremble
In the stillness of the air

The earth cracks
The rocks shift
And houses shudder
In a tremor of despair

The crust splits
The trees snap
And mountains crumble
With the tumbling of the world

Earthquake!
Earthquake!

What can stand in the path
Of the gathering storm?
Who can hold up his head
When the skies rain stones?

Earthquake!
Earthquake!

Where once there stood a forest
Broken branches lie
Where once there stood a village
Shattered stonework sighs
Where once there stood a mountain
Darkling dust clouds rise

In the eye of the storm
Demons ride
Warriors of the night
Shut out the light
Of the streaming sun

Earthquake!
Earthquake!

Moving, shifting
Falling, cracking
Lurching, trembling
Crumbling, breaking
Howling, bursting
Splitting wide…

In a broken toothed smile
The shattered earth gapes
Like some crazy spinning top
The drunken world stops

Earthquake!
Earthquake!
Earthquake!

The ground shakes
The stones move
And branches tremble
In the stillness of the air.

The Legend of Mindobamba

In a time, upon a time of long ago,
Three hundred miles and more from Chimborazo,
In a place of snowy waste and mountains tall,
A valley deep of pastures green where eagles call.

It was the time, the day of Mindobamba,
When God spoke and raised his fearsome hammer,
Arauca shook and men looked up in wonder
As mountains fell with searing roar of thunder.

Come hear the legend of the country of the blind,
Of fortunes and mystery, time out of mind.

In a time, upon a time of long ago,
There lay a path that opened to the world
Where brave men might come through rocky ways of snow
To pastures green beyond a jagged gorge.

It was the time, the day of Mindobamba,
When daylight fled before night's dreadful banner,
Water boiled and fish floated in the river
And houses fell as stonework broke asunder.

Come hear the legend of the country of the blind,
Of fortunes and mystery, time out of mind.

On a day, upon a day of long ago,
There fell a man from the sky on clouds of snow,
From that place of icy waste he bore a bar
Of silver fine and riches great from country far.

It was the time, the day of Mindobamba,
When God spoke and raised his fearsome hammer,
A hero fell and told us tales of wonder,
Of blind men lost in avalanche of thunder.

Come hear the legend of the country of the blind,
Of silver and mystery, wealth out of mind,
Come hear the legend of the country of the blind,
Of fortunes and mystery, lost in time.

Swing that Hammer

Chains on my legs,
Chains on my hands,
Walkin' together
Led by the Man.

Don't see no mother,
Children don't come,
Ain't nothin' here
But rocks and the sun.

Grit in my eyes,
Dust in my mouth,
Rocks to the north
And stones to the south.

Swingin' that hammer,
Smashin' them stones,
That ole Uncle Sam
He breakin' my bones.

I got them smashin' the stones blues,
I got them scrapin' the bones shoes,
Chains are adraggin'
Sun is aburnin'
Men all apoundin'
Smashin' the mountain,
I got them smashin' the stones blues,
I got them scrapin' the bones shoes.

Swing that hammer!

Chains on my legs,
Hammer 'n my hand,
Workin' together
Led by the Man.

Blisters apoppin'
Hands torn and rough,
Stones for the crunchin'
I sure had enough.

Lookin' around me
What can I see?
Sweatin' and boilin'
I wanna be free.

Swingin' that hammer,
Smashin' them stones,
That ole Uncle Sam
He breakin'my bones.

I got them dancin' railroad shoes,
I got them singin' jailbird blues,
Smash that mountain!

Swing that hammer,
Smash them stones,
Poundin' together,
Breakin' them bones!
I got them smashin'the bones shoes,
I got them smashin'…
      -   keep on bashin'
I got them smashin' the stones…
      -   blues.

The Song of the World

I am dust
You are dust
We are dust
All flesh is dust

In the beginning
When the world was naught
And rocks were razor sharp
The wild wind howled

The cold wind howls
And nothing moves
Save dust upon the rocks

Comes the hand of God

God's finger moves
And rests upon
The razor sharp
Of the virgin rock

And all is smooth
And all is still

In the heart of the rock
Lies a waiting world

Overhead
Stretches smooth
The roof of the world
Feel the roof of the world
The arch of heaven

And from it falls
The dew and the rock
It is our blood
It is our life

The gifts of God upon the earth
The water of life

And thus is made the world

But I am dust
You are dust
We are dust
All flesh is dust

And the made world waits
For nothing moves
Nor drinks the dew of life
Empty is the world that waits
No breath drinks
The new-made air

Listen to the sound
Of hoof and claw
Gathering sinew
Surging here

The creatures come
The sound of feet upon the rock
The shudder of life upon the earth

And thus is made the world.

In the Country of the Blind

In the country of the blind
The one-eyed man is king,
He who rules with iron hand
Will control the people.

In the fortress of this land
Shall I build my kingdom,
All who come before my throne
Will submit their freedom.

They will bow their bended knee
And proclaim their service,
I shall wear the golden crown,
Monarch of the mountains.

From the coffers of these hills
The silver ore will flow,
I shall sit on jewelled throne
Sole lord of this Eden.

He who wields the sword of power
Knows when the hour is ripe,
For there is a tide of fate
When chance of glory comes.

Now is the hour
Now is the time
Mine is the power
This is my time.

In the country of the blind
The one-eyed man is king,
In the valley of the blind
My sight shall make me king.

Now is the hour
Now is the time
Mine is the power
This is my time.

The Spinning Song
Echoes and Whispers

In the silent house a young girl's spinning,
Weaving threads upon the loom of time,
If she listens she can hear the ripples,
Patterns of her life in teasing rhyme.

Passing through her fingers,
Drifting through her dreaming,
Whispers of tomorrow,
Echoes of what might have been.

In the dreaming house a young girl's spinning
Softest linen for her trothing day.
In the springtime fields her young man's singing
Carols for a life of loving ways.

Whispers, echoes,
Passing through her fingers,
Echoes, whispers,
Drifting through her dreams.

In the busy house a mother's spinning
Warmest clothing for a girl and boy,
On the firestone hearth supper's simmering,
Emblems of a life of homely joy.

Passing through her fingers,
Drifting through her dreaming,
Whispers of tomorrow,
Echoes of what might have been.

In the sombre house a woman's spinning
Shroud cloth plain for loving husband cold,
While she spins her bitter tears are falling,
Keening for a life that's now grown old.

Whispers, echoes,
Passing through her fingers,
Echoes, whispers,
Drifting through her dreams.

In the silent house a young girl's spinning,
Weaving threads upon the loom of time,
If she listens she can hear the ripples,
Patterns of her life in teasing rhyme.

The Morning of the Last Day

On the morning of the last day
I gaze into the rising sun,
Like an angel in golden armour
It floods the land with fire and light.

There I see a flash of crystal
And shining colours in the rocks,
Mountain peaks stand sharp and jagged,
A giant's teeth biting the sky.

In the valley dark shadows cling,
A shifting purple, deepening blue,
Creeping slowly through field and meadow,
The darkness lifts with coming day.

I see the mountains tower above me,
I see the bright light of the golden sun,
I see the valley plunged into shadow
And from tomorrow, darkness awaits me.

The light or the dark,
The dark or the light,
Magic of sunrise
Or an endless night?

On the morning of the last day
I gaze into the rising sun,
Like an angel in golden armour
It floods the land with fire and light.

Like a king or conquering hero
I fell from the height of the sun,
Bringing gifts of sight and wisdom
And found that she was the only one.

I see the mountains tower above me,
I see the bright light of the golden sun,
I see the valley plunged into shadow
And from tomorrow, darkness awaits me.

The light or the dark,
The dark or the light,
Magic of sunrise
Or an endless night?

Climbing the Steps

Turning your back on the dark of the night,
Scaling the heights and taking your chances,
Climbing the steps of imagination,
Cresting the last ridge to gaze at the sun.

Forcing your footsteps forever onwards,
Breaking the chains that tie you to earth,
Climbing the steps of imagination,
Cresting the last ridge to gaze at the sun.

Hand on hand and you're reaching for the stars,
One step wrong and you'll never climb again.

Saying goodbye to those who have loved you,
Knowing tomorrow you'll see the sun rise,
Climbing the steps of imagination,
Cresting the last ridge to gaze at the sun.

Hand on hand and you're reaching for the stars,
One step wrong and you'll never climb again.

Turning your back on the dark of the night,
Scaling the heights and taking your chances,
Climbing the steps of imagination,
Cresting the last ridge to gaze at the sun.

Songs from *The Mysteries*

Everything

Everything you do,
You do for me.

Fathers of the children
Understand the pain,
Mothers of the children
Watch the blood red stain,
The sacrifice of children slain
Running down the palace walls,
Fields of mud and tainted gutters.

Hammer and nail,
Blood and white bone,
Someone's lost child
Slowly dying.

Everything you do,
You do for me.

Miracle

It's a miracle
It's a miracle
As the lame man walks
And the blind man sees
For the light shines on
As the power grows strong
It's a miracle
It's a miracle
And the dumb man speaks
And the leper heals
For the light shines on
As the power grows strong
It's a miracle
It's a miracle
And the dead man lives
Yes the dead man lives
For the light shines on
As the power grows strong
It's a miracle
It's a miracle.

The Wheel is Turning

And the threads of time
Spin on heaven's loom,
For the wheel is turning
And the days are burning
As the web of time
Weaves the voice of doom.

And the hands of man
Sift the sands of time,
For the wheel is turning
And the years are burning
As the deeds of man
Flood the plains of time.

Sift the grains
Through your hand,
Build your house
On shifting sand,
Cast the dice
Lay waste the land,
Don't look now
Just play your hand.

For the wheel spins round
In this vale of tears,
Can't you hear the sound
Blast the empty years?

And the heart of man
Feeds on gold and blood,
For the wheel is turning
And the days are burning
As the ways of man
Pierce the heart of God.

III – The Ghost in the Machine

Route Sixty-Six Revisited

When I came down to Etruria
back in nineteen hundred and sixty-six
on my journey to university at Keele,

I did not find classical civilization,
just the smoking bottle kilns of the Potteries,
the sheds and stacks of Wedgewood and Spode

and an ever-present smear of grey and black,
the unfathomable depths of the old canal,
a gash in the city's arteries and heart.

But back in sixty-six some things changed,
Dylan went electric at the Albert Hall,
a new youthful eye sparked the sixties

and the air was gradually scoured clear,
the scum and viscous sludge drained,
the hedgerows replanted with hawthorn and alder,

the floating pennywort, nettles and parsleys regrafted
and the roach and carp, the voles and damselflies
reclaimed the wastelands and waterways,

while the green mating lights of the glow-worms
rekindled hope sometime after I left Etruria,
heading out along the way on route sixty-six.

Arlecchino in Aleppo: Down that Dusty Road

This is not a time for inspiration,
I am not rooted here,
an appendage, assemblage,
the barren fruits of earth stretch
withered,
every last pip ground to dust
and only the fool carries
the watering can
singing an old pilgrim song.

This is a time for measure and for weight,
for categorising,
analysing and weaponising,
the hollow streets stretch
wasted,
every gesture forensically examined
and only the fool laughs,
swings his body
chanting an old pilgrim lay.

Time swerves around time,
definitions coalesce
and heat and cold are but the arbiters
of the complementary,
the well has been drained dry,
mind is out of joint
and only the recrimination
of blood remains,
drifting down the dusty road
to the insistent rhythm
of an old pilgrim hymn.

Between Dream and Sweetheart

now the war is no longer
top billing on
the evening news
we may in time forget

the bombed theatre
at Mariupol
with hundreds ground
to dust in the cellar

the Tochka-U rocket
blasting the apartment block
the pregnant woman
with her legs blown off

the bodies piled with tyres
the mass graves
between the villages
of Dream and Sweetheart

but I will not forget
the sand-bagged
statue of the poet
and the image of

the child in a grey anorak
and yellow bobble hat
staring wide-eyed
with his palm pressed

against the cold glass
of the carriage window
as the train shudders
into motion

The Boatman's Reel
After John Armstrong, Crossing the Styx

Since words are words and the word is all there is,
I have no choice but to weave such a web,
weave an intricate mystery of air,
invite you to participate, forbid you to share;
and I am tired of acting the boatman
rowing to schedule across the dark river,
touting tickets on the wilderness edge,
harvesting coins from unseeing eyes.

Time stretches, the relentless Appian Way,
backcloth of dust, slate to write figures on;
agglomerate of atoms, speck of consciousness,
flickers and gasps, expostulates and is gone.

Sour seaway, path the prophet traverses,
links patriarch Paul blinded in Damascus
and exiled Dante brooding in Sienna;
the gentleman's coat of arms, newly bought,
floats as driftwood on the storm-beaten shore,
while the wild air keens an ancient elegy
in the desert, precincts of Elsinore.

Hoisting the blades from the water, I incant
hollow dustwords to comfort and succour you,
for the stream that swells the ocean augurs a sea-change:
let the unfinished requiem begin
and the lacrimosa drift across the swirling waves.

Pins and Needles

How many angels on a pinhead
　　　　　　　　　　　　how many pins says the guru
but the addict counts the pricks
　　　　　　　　　　　　　　and points the finger straight at you

pricks and points and pins and angels
　　　　　　　　　　　　　　many sharp-pronged wounds incise
wield the scalpel doctor oh my brother
　　　　　　　　　　　　　　　carve the flesh for the world to view

see the precise needle cicatrise
　　　　　　　　　　　but wouldn't you rather
　　　　　　　　　　　　　　　　　stop than go farther
and watch
　　　　　　　those shimmering angels hypnotically entice
　　　　　　　　　　　　　　light and life and you yes you

Echoes

Bells that toll through the snow
confirm the absence of the sun,
white powder and grey dust
trace the way we have gone;
clouds that stretch across the sky today
form the backcloth of the skyscape,
russet and orange, violet and green,
shapeshift across your hazy sight.

Roar of the city and gusts of the downs
are smothered in gathering stillness
and the faces, pallid or bronzed,
crumble to nothing in your dreams;
do you tire of these gaudy illuminations,
and do you tire of yourself, child of neon,
child of clay, child of the evening,
does your light refract in stuttering echoes
and return in sharp fragments
as you watch the faces in the room?

She has stood in a hall of mirrors,
arms full of flowers,
posing attitudes gracefully
and failed to choose her image,
stepped from frame to frame
and passed distantly into the evening,
hear the echo, the echo,
self and self echoing through the hollow room.

The Ghost in the Machine

Descartes was, one might say, somewhat eccentric,
lethargic too – he never rose before noon
except to perform for an exacting queen
who desired an elucidation of the cosmos.
Needless to say, he left the court in haste,
muttering oaths about the land of Gustavus,
retiring to the comfort of an old Dutch stove.
Very soon, he died; pleurisy and cold killed him.

A little later, the revolution was over,
his proof of God dismissed or ignored,
others came who pronounced the death of the spirit:
clocks in their hands and utopia in their hearts,
they chanted wild slogans of man supreme.
Later still a new barrenness settled on the land,
some began to murmur that it was all a mistake,
but the co-ordinates of the soul had long gone missing.

Calliope

taut tensile strength of sensual
    body string flow
                                caught
in the binary pull of experience
    mindsprung into beauty

fragile filigree she swings you
    breathlessly grasping
                        at any and no
human straw
    mind and body sadly separate

incantatory dreamer no realm
    of fantasy
                    unknown unknowing
lovely too
    also a construct of our times

wondering and credulous
    black/white frame for verbal leaps
                      dancing high or low
split
    an image shimmering in a universe
        of mirrors

Nocturne

As I watch you sleeping,
see your breasts rise and fall,
I hear the tree moaning,
grasping in the wind
and clasping in the air
as your hand clutches the sheet.

You, you are silent restful,
far from the tree that groans,
you cannot hear it raking the sky
and I, telescope of all
sounds and sense impressions,
am seared by their call.

Your flesh is hot and burning,
your brow white, white hot –
you stir in your sleep –
but the wind, it is there
still curling
through the tree and the sky.

The wind, it will cool you,
infiltrate your sleep
and you will carry
the imprint of the night
tomorrow, when you wake.

Spinning Time

Van the Man's singing on the radio
about playing Russian roulette with the mind
and I'm there way back when a long time ago,
gambling with the heart and dealing aces blind.
We met at some smoky party one night
before the world was fixed and set in stone,
but we parted under the blue station light,
heading out along those distant tracks alone.
Now time has flowed down that restless river
and plenty of driftwood has washed to the sea,
but the only branches that I remember
were hewn from the trunk of the living tree
and every throw of the dice has led me to this:
the spinning live bullet is triggered by a kiss.

The Bargain
After Julian of Norwich

She offered him an almond in exchange for his silver bike.
Nuts, he said, do you think I'm some kind of prize walnut?
There are wheels within wheels, she mysteriously replied,
and you never know where a fine almond will take you.

What's so special about a tiny nut? he brusquely asked,
where will your almond take me that my shiny bike won't go?
Follow your instincts she suggested, leaning across his handlebars
and casually placing her slender hand upon his bicycle bell.

Almonds are what you make of them, she smoothly said,
you can suck, lick, crunch or swallow it whole in one go,
grind it, roast it, sugar it, pour sunflower oil upon it,
draw it, paint it, frame it, juggle it or plant it in a pot.

Fire up your imagination, she teasingly said, or stay
forever pedalling your wheels on the treadmill of life,
chasing a dirt-track dream to nowhere. She smiled
and offered him her almond in exchange for his silver bike.

Pay & Display

Pay & display
that's the kind of invitation
that seems worth thinking about

so ok
everything has its price
negotiate the ticket

and hey
you can launch your boat
pack your case – grab hat & coat

you're away
tripping the light fantastic
strutting your mean-street stuff

glamour queen, sight unseen
you knock 'em all dead, baby
they grovel at your high-heeled feet

or rev up that star-spinning engine
burning the gas through drop-jawed
head-turning boulevard

Superman skydiving to rescue
Batman arriving in the slick of time
Spiderman sticky-webfooting down

some other kind of display suit you better?
acumen and gravitas
the world tripping on the tip of your tongue

the world's your oyster, buster
whatever flash you can muster
let it loose – but hold on just a

mo
is it possible to let it all go
with the drop of a coin and heave-ho

with
all the old inhibitions
the hand on the shoulder
doubt in the night-time
can I or can't I prevarications?

maybe
it's trickier than it looks
this bright wink of an eye come-on

we know
the old stories of Faustian bargains
darkened deed and whole-soul steal

it really isn't that easy
so as you stand
before the meter
gauging the risk
of renting a few hours
for your special delight

you better ask yourself the right question
not have you paid and displayed
but would you if you could?

The Examination
After Kafka

It is impossible, he said,
waking to the insistent glare
of the torch in his eyes,
I cannot tell you what you want to know.

The wheel of the rack turned,
the leaves floated crisply in the wind
and a crack of light seeped stealthily
into the room.

I am what I am,
I am what I say,
there is no more,

that rock does not bear my imprint,
the sands shift constantly,
the tree sap oozes at the teeth of the axe
and the stars turn; in this,
where is the room?

You are breathing over the inspection glass
and Bonhoeffer died many years ago,
come speak, and let us trade in our abstractions
for the feel of the concrete,
for the touch of the instrument which is here.

I reiterate,
all is flux,
a cascading, inconceivable whirl
of cosmic particles which may,
or may not, be real;
it is the hour glass of Holbein,
the cold touch of the unknown hand
when you are alone at midnight,
it is the pulse of the womb-tissue

issuing you,
it is perhaps the conjugation
but that will later pillory you

now I ask you –
(and he peremptorily stretched
 a metaphorical finger)
what do you mean by your question?

Come, come,
you twist words into ancient strands,
the greying cleric, perhaps a pardoner,
would tell you as much
but at least with a dose of sauce,
you answer the question.

And again the wheel of the rack turned,
the leaves floated crisply in the wind
and a crack of light seeped stealthily
into the room.

This then, is your answer,
I will say no more,
I can say no more,
the muscle that moves the hand
is the spring that turns the wheel,
is the tendon which is ripped,
is the throat from which the scream is torn

        but that is not all
for the pain is mine alone,
mine is the sawdust from the desecration of the tree,
is the individual stamen of the apple blossom
        the pain is mine alone.

The wheel of the rack turned
and turned again;
the queue advanced by one place.

Conditional Tense

I have heard it said
        that it is only important
                to preserve
a pretence of participation
                being episcopal
of course I am at liberty to dispute this
        for though it may be written
             that all our greatest figures
                were anti-clerics
        I beg leave to differ

I am
                the archbishop
I eat
                lamb and muffins
they curdle my soul substance
                crunch
my pew-honey but leave it sufficiently
                whole
for select acquaintances to finger
                & even absorb
        after evensong

        after evensong
when I walk
                pace & pontificate
the screaming stone
                pillars & orifices
of my domain
                confront the gargoyle
mutter obscenities under my breath
                and use my staff
to select the hymn
                and interest

the recalcitrant virgin

                       who waits

        musingly

                       on any stone steps

catching teardrops

                       and mandrakes

and the opportunity for blood worship

                              that

which didn't come

                           when

the blacksmith or the courtier cavorted

                   phantasmagorically

I don

                      the implications

        of

my office

                      after evensong

I comfort the deviant beggar

                     & commiserate

with the cosmic flashes of the schizophrenic

                     incipient of course

        who
        actually believes

                that

a utopia

        god–given or man–made

                awaits

the sincerity

        of the scholarly/libertine/ascetic/
        witchdoctor/scientist/ritual-reciter/
        poet/politician/artist/eccentric engineer/
        intense lavatory attendant/ astronomer/
        stud-farm porn-star/botanist/
        linguist-cum-prophet/ even archbishop

I do not laugh

                        in my
          robes
                      they entertain
even the doubts of the revolutionary theoriser
          my episcopal wine/water/coffee/words
                  can accommodate

          I am
after a fashion a shepherd with a conditional flock
          after all
                  there is always
          veneration

so
                  my political intimations
& intuitive
                  if unvoiced
          reservations
about a linear history
                  can resolve
themselves
                  outside of mysticism

          conditionally
all
          is
                  tentative
          even

the hallucinatory
                  can be integrative

the altars of penance/worship/hope/alleviating despair
          beyond all
                  are plankton profligate

those putti had more vision in their conception
                    than your
                              perverse

                                        coloured
macro–biotic slides

                                but that of course is not a
                                definitive statement
                                on reconsideration
                                all barriers are
                                    the constructs of a
                                    delimiting
                                    pseudo
                                    yet proud
singularity

                    concluding
I uphold

                              my chalice & vestments

 candles and the devil are my blancmange
                    the politic niceties of my experience
the convoluting apparitions
                                        stewed
                    in the heat of epistemological beds
  with homilies and imprecations hurled from the highest spire

                    I am

                                    the archbishop
and I bristle with delight

                                at experience

                    of negatives of the world

The Beggar and the Bowl

The dead leaves sprawl in the gutter,
my seventieth summer has come
and it is autumn,
the tapping stick of the blind man
and the begging bowl of age and winter
await me. Is it not written
within the bark of these trees,
in the very stones of these streets,
that all must abdicate?
My seventieth summer has come
and the leaves are labels,
the light is a sticking pin.
With age I see the contradictions
as the dry sticks beat
the wooden alms bowl
in a harsh tattoo
through these long-shadowed streets.

Requiem

Go away, go away Satyr, Sylph, Dryad,
Cyclops; go Ariel, Minotaur, Orion, Caliban,
Back to the world you should never have left.
I have played my last tune,
See my notes are dissolute,
You cannot dance to them now –
They are lost in the laughter of time.
Do not stay to grieve, your tears
Are wasted in the greater sorrow,
Leave now, there is nothing for you here,
Go away, leave now,
    I cannot assuage you –
        Soon, it will be finished.

There was a time for joy and for exultation,
A time for earth, for planting and for growing,
An occasion to sing, to dance
And to melt into mourning.
Now the time is almost past,
It is good that it should be so.

Why do you linger,
        Have I not told you
                It is over?
  There is only time now for dissolution.

The tree disowns the root, the root disowns the soil,
For what was once soil is now only dust,
The wind scatters the dust and a yellow bone
Whiteness lies on greyness, crawls under the silkworm;
Nettles grow in vineyards
And a strange black shadow
Hangs black in the sky,
The executioner threatens the hangman
For the earth is very old now,
And it cannot last.

Go now, Hera, Nefertiti, Beatrice,
Aphrodite, Freya, Cleopatra, Helen –
Your visions are too bright,
They do not belong to this world,
Which is sunken deeper than material mire.
Your eyes gleam in vain,
The marble sublimity
Of your flesh, which once
Gave immortality or madness,
Is lost and gone, invalid
And negated now.
This time is not yours
To impersonate with perfection;
It has its own unspeakable,
Inconceivable, unknowable beauty,
It dissolves you like acid – you cannot
Intervene, or even watch, bear witness.
See, even the spectre of Tiresias fades.

So how can you
                    Incarnate polarity
Expect to be manifest
                    At a time like this?
You have outworn the earth, but go, leave now,
    Sleep in peace.

Concrete crumbles to sand, cement blows
On the desert wind, roads run nowhere
And the signposts shimmer with a turquoise hue;
Jewels that glowed in the statue's eye
Burn brown with rust on the lake bed.
Tumultuous spirit-river,
Emblem of growth and of man,
The end and the beginning,
The beginning and the end
Are upon you, and you are gone.

Come, the multitude of your voices,
Music your own calls you and you must leave,
Cezanne, Sophocles, Dante and Keats,
Masaccio, Mahler, Blake and Messiaen.
The elements dissolve before your eyes,
Your art that sought a higher actuality,
Meaning beyond the mind, mind beyond the soul
And soul beyond the meaning
Encoils about you;

For this darkness, which is not night,
Will allow no perception, essence or reality.
You have sung, but those that absorbed you,
Gave you life, hung your script
For eternity, are gone.
They cannot hear you now, comes
The new and terrible sound of the abyss.

So turn away
              Do not apprehend
Leave in your glory

For you reached the heights of man
And cannot withstand this; turn away,
                              Go now,
    For the hour of earth is done.

The Masks of Anarchy
(With apologies to P.B. Shelley)

The song of the Thames-side boatmen
As they sail the ship of state
Rings out across the choppy waters
While the winds of pestilence blow,
Row, boys, row!

The helmsman stands at the rudder
Surveying his motley crew,
Tousled blond hair all askew,
Give it all you've got, boys,
Row, boys, row!

The virus may rage in China
And Italy's hospitals are full,
The Spaniards are on their knees
But we're still playing football,
Row, boys, row!

The scientists say the death-count
Is heading for the skies,
So jam on the brakes boys
A U-turn is looking wise,
Row, boys, row!

And everyone's confined to barracks
With ambulances lined in a row
Treating patients in the car park
While hospital wards overflow,
Row, boys, row!

We're dishing out contracts like confetti,
Ordering PPE from Pestfix,
Aprons and masks from Turkey
And gloves from Nigel's aunt,
Row, boys, row!